Written in the Kitchen

Poems from the life and imagination of a housewife

To Susan

with my very best wishes –

Betty Akin-Flenley.

Elizabeth Akin-Flenley

authorHOUSE®

AuthorHouse™ UK Ltd.
500 Avebury Boulevard
Central Milton Keynes, MK9 2BE
www.authorhouse.co.uk
Phone: 08001974150

Published by AuthorHouse   2/13/2012

ISBN: 978-1-4389-5262-8 (sc)

in
day

called *Because*

my legs and
much of the

nitial
ation and the
ng one; taking

ire everything
y's grandson
d the project,
; experience,
as an actor in

lack of
nd modern
helped to

raft had to be
hen sent back
oyal Mail
be made."
en part of the
n however. It's
nd
bringing

ry excited to
have always
of the family,
es for other

ord in 1965
d John Akin.
ed later that
s aircraft
ault and
on July 6.

NEW VENTURE: Elizabeth Akin-Flenley with her book of poems which has just been published

PICTURE: Kevin Bates

Betty's sons Tim and Michael both live nearby and her daughters Trisha and Lizzy now live in Devon.

The collection *Written in the Kitchen: Poems from the Life and Imagination of a Housewife*, is currently available for sale online with Waterstones, Borders and other major marketplaces including Amazon.

pupils pays off for A

memories

Betty's book is o
time for 80th bir

Bathford resident Elizabeth Akin-Flenley marked her 80th birthday recently with the release of her debut poetry collection, *Written in the Kitchen: Poems from the Life and Imagination of a Housewife*.

The collection totals more than 30 poems which are imaginative, emotive and witty.

Some are serious, some mournful and some are just right for children. They paint the pictures of a life through the hard times and the happy times.

Individually the poems illustrate Betty's theatricality, love and reflection of life, appreciation of nature and the countryside and over-imagination for just about everything.

"At no stage did I ever expect my little poems to find their way into print", says Betty. "They were simply a means of enjoyment and would just pop into my head. I would jot them down on a piece of paper and put them in the kitchen drawer."

Betty is at the centre of large extended family with four children, nine grandchildren and one great grandchild.

Betty continued: "I suppose the birth of the home computer started the initial organisation of my poems from a messy pile of scribblings. My daughter Lizzy typed them all up for me from my original copies over 10 years ago. Then, many years later,

A new book of poetry by Elizabeth Akin-Flenley bypasses the technological age

my grandson Jamie decided something more significant should be made of them.

"After approaching some self-publishing companies, he will now also manage the sales and promotion for me. I just look forward to sending each copy on its way with a smile."

That smile extends to a commitment to personally sign requests, pack and post each copy that is ordered.

"I don't expect for one minute to sell many copies", quips Betty. "But those that I do sell, I shall look forward to packing up myself, walking down the hill with my little dog and sending them on their way."

Her dog, Bernie, a black miniature Poodle, even takes a featured role in a couple of poems. "Bernie crops up in a couple of my poems,

parti
I'm S
"He
about
produ
The
concep
releas
almo
"We
was ri
Jamie,
with li
alongsi
Londor
"My g
sympat
technol
lengthe
"Each
printed,
to Bath.
before p
He add
charm o
been a v
hand-cra
hours of
"I know
see the p
been a ch
finally re
people to
Betty m
with RAI
John was
year whe
suffered a
crashed n

Hard work in tracking dov

Foreword

When I first started writing poems many years ago, I never for one moment thought I would see them in print and yet here I am trying to write a foreword to my own little book!

I am now in my seventies and I am happy to say, very fit. My family, in an affectionate way, call me eccentric and I think I probably am; but I believe at my age one is entitled to be. Also, one can get away with all kinds of things in the name of eccentricity!

This will undoubtedly be my only book but I have gained much pleasure in collecting all my poems together from around the house. I hope you, the reader, can share in the pleasure that they brought to my family and me.

Acknowledgements

I wish to thank Tim, Trisha, Michael and Lizzie for their patient encouragement of my poetic endeavours!

I also wish to thank my grandson Jamie, because without his determination and perseverance my little book would still be a bundle of papers in my kitchen drawer.

Finally, I am grateful to Anna for her dedicated assistance in the production process.

Written in the Kitchen

Contents

Frustration

One wonders what possible reason
The clerk of the weather would find
For messing up our winter season,
And making it sunny and kind.

His store of snow must be enormous,
He's built it up over the years;
Why can't he pop down and inform us
Why our share is so in arrears?

So long we have waited and wondered,
Our sledges all ready to go;
But someone up there must have blundered,
And simply forgotten our snow.

So back in the sheds go our sledges,
Once more it has turned out the same;
We can't scoop the snow off the hedges
For snowballs or similar game.

Each winter our faces are glowing,
Our noses turn really quite red;
But that's not because it's been snowing,
The sun has been shining instead.

So here is a lesson for learning,
Forget winter ever began;
Smoothe oil on to stop yourself burning,
And soak up the sun while you can.

The Country Call

I don't want to be in the city today,
The tarmac and buildings offend me;
I'd much rather be in a lane far away,
With countryside things to attend me.

I'd like to have birds singing high in the trees,
Or feeding themselves in the hedges;
I'd like to have fields stretch as far as I please,
With pale sleeping hills at the edges.

I'd like to have cows standing under a tree,
With cooling shade dappled around them,
Their tails swinging high as they try to keep free
From insects that constantly hound them.

And there will be grasses sweet smelling and tall,
Sun bleached and with cobwebs suspended,
Where spiders wait patiently poised for the call,
Then grab their prey as was intended.

A stream would be nice for my road-weary feet,
Clear water to freshen my feelings;
Small fish have no thoughts of the rich and elite,
Nor yet of industrial dealings.

All nature is here, every inch, every mile,
Attending to natural matters;
No letters to finish, no papers to file,
Where nothing rings, whistles or clatters.

I would like to be in that lane far away,
With countryside things all around me;
But I have to be in the city today,
Where buildings and tarmac have bound me.

Total Rubbish

My head said to my arm
"It might cause some alarm
If I were yellow, you were green.
A jolly fellow to be seen.
It couldn't do much harm".

My arm said to my head
"I think it should be said
That I prefer the colour blue.
The colour green just will not do.
Could I be blue instead?"

My other arm cried "Oh!
'Twould make a lovely show
If I were orange—very bright;
'Twould give my hand a fearful fright
And make my fingers glow!"

My head said to my leg
"Do answer me I beg,
What colour would you like to be?"
My leg said "I must ask my knee,
Do ask my brother Peg".

My other leg replied
"I really can't decide.
I think the pretty colour puce
Would give me such a good excuse
To walk about with pride!"

And then they laughed and laughed,
And called each other daft.
Then not another word was said.
And so we floated up to bed
Aboard a hovercraft.

Waiting

Nothing has pitched yet up there on the plain,
The top of the plain is quite bare;
All of which means that last shower was rain,
There still is no snow in the air.

Roads down our way are all dark, shining wet,
They clatter and crunch when they sound;
Nature has not given snow to us yet,
There's nothing but rain on the ground.

View from My Window

Against a tapestry of evening clouds,
Soft grey and pink against a softer blue,
The west-bound sun with golden light enshrouds
October's world of warm autumnal hue.

My window shows a rich and varied scene
Of meadows, hills, a multitude of trees,
All changing now from shades of summer's green,
Obeying winter's call upon the breeze.

A lazy snake of chimney smoke climbs high,
Provoking thoughts of burning logs and wine,
Declaring it has been a perfect day,
And promising tomorrow will be fine.

A bonfire too burns someone's garden waste,
The smoke hangs low, not drifting anywhere;
One feels the neighbours must, with frantic haste,
Be grabbing washing from the unclean air.

As I enjoy my view as every day
The burning sun is sinking out of sight;
While black birds seeking roosts fly far away,
The world prepares to greet another night.

Observations

In human life there's so much speed
Acquiring all we think we need.
But as we dash by car or plane
When do we listen to the rain?

We're captives of computer screens,
Of telephones and fax machines.
That being so, when do our eyes
Observe the sunset fill the skies?

To beat the clock we toil and fret,
We have a "deadline to be met".
We smell success, maybe it's ours,
But have we ever smelt the flowers?

The years must come, the years must go,
But it's the beauty of the snow;
The wind, the rain, the evening sun,
That stays with us 'til life is done.

We knew the sun was always there,
But did we ever really care?
We knew it rained, we knew it blew,
But then we had so much to do.

It takes a few advancing years
To still the race, to wipe the tears
And clear our eyes to see the truth
We never noticed in our youth.

Utter Nonsense

"Do you want one or sixty-three?"
The purple monkey said to me.
I crossed my legs and scratched my nose,
And played piano with my toes.
And then I said "You see;
If I had one it's not enough,
And really they're so very rough,
Not suitable for tea."
The monkey, looking very hot,
Said "Don't you talk a load of rot!"
And scampered up a tree.

Upon a Death

Sing on sweet bird.
I hear your melancholy tones.
I hear them ring,
And when you sing
There's sadness in my bones.

Your life was part of ours.
We heard your song
Together in the sunshine,
Warm and long,
Amid the flowers;
And now the sun and you remain
To bring me pain.

A Knock at the Door

"Good morning, I'm seeking a fam'ly of bears."
"Oh, are you my dear? Well, they're living upstairs.
The father is such a remarkable chap.
The mother? You just want to sit on her lap.
The children are sweet; do go up if you wish.
They're painted up there on my pot-pourri dish!"

Because I'm Seventy-Three

An early hour to leave my bed,
Cold water splash to clear my head.
Consult the list of things to do
Then get to work and work straight through.
Yes, that is how it used to be;
Not any more, I'm seventy-three.

I do not rise to greet the dawn,
I do not feel at all reborn.
I do the jobs that must be done
But where's the element of fun?
For that is how it used to be;
Not any more, I'm seventy-three.

There's just my little dog and me,
We live alone quite happily.
There isn't much for us to do,
No need to daily polish through.
For that is how it used to be;
Not any more, I'm seventy-three.

Sometimes we have a lazy day
And let the hours pass away.
No one will come and criticise,
Our home is lovely in our eyes.
And that is how it's going to be.
It suits me well at seventy-three.

Dark Wind of the Night

Where are you going dark wind of the night?
Are you just torturing my garden trees?
Black silhouettes tossing wild at their height.
Are you tormenting more branches than these?

I hear meandering pin-pricks of rain
Burst to a battering borne there by you,
Swirling across my small piece of terrain,
Throwing your weight at my window anew.

Still for a while as you muster once more,
Ready to throw sheets of rain at my walls,
Hurl round the corner and howl at my door,
Thrashing and splashing from merciless squalls.

I lie abed where it's soft and it's warm,
I crave no comforting, I need no light.
I am secure in the arms of the storm,
I shall sleep soundly, dark wind of the night.

As with an island protected by sea
I have no threatening foe in my sight.
I have the strength of the storm shielding me,
I am at peace with this passionate night.

The House of Memories

Did you see that little house back there a few yards from the road?
With the evening sun upon it, did you see the way it glowed?
I am sure it must have been there for two hundred years or more,
With its low and latticed windows and its heavy wooden door.

Did you see the mass of roses climbing up against the wall?
And the hollyhocks and marigolds, delphiniums and all?
One would think that these were planted to reflect the times long gone,
To ensure it's all in keeping, even though the world's moved on.

But I much prefer my own idea that nothing here has changed
And that not a single flower head had ever been arranged;
That the ghosts of long-dead gardeners no longer called to toil,
Simply watch until the time is right then call them from the soil.

For to me this is a house of ghosts, of many laughs and tears,
That come echoing through passages across so many years.
And one ponders on the sad times that these same old walls have seen,
And one thinks, too, of the happy times there surely must have been.

Then one wonders just how many hands have touched these aged walls,
With their owners passing through the door when making friendly calls.
Then one thinks about the clothes they wore and where they stood in life;
One example I envisage is a farmer and his wife.

And then maybe silken crinolines swept through the garden gate
To the road which was in those days in a dusty, stony state;
Then the ladies and their chaperones might wait there for a coach
Which, with hot and steaming horses, would so very soon approach.

But inside this house I picture very clearly in my mind
Just the very kind of furnishings that I'd expect to find.
There'd be dark and polished tables and white linen here and there
And a home-made lacy cushion in a high-backed wooden chair.

There would be a cosy inglenook with logs piled close at hand
With a mantelpiece above it and a candle in a stand.
There would be some pretty pieces made of china and of glass,
And some uncompleted needlepoint to help the evenings pass.

And the visitor would notice just the faintest smell of soot,
And the darkly patterned carpet, somewhat threadbare underfoot.
In a corner by the window stands a fine grandfather clock
With its ornamental casing and a ponderous 'tick tock'.

Now, I'm sure if I should enter there and walk into the hall,
An electric carpet sweeper would be plugged into the wall,
With the television blaring, if I needed further proof—
Though I had observed an aerial was fastened to the roof.

But it's time I put my wild imagination out of bounds;
I've created a museum in this cottage and its grounds.
I will leave it to its gadgets and the wish to modernise,
While I go and find another little house to organise.

Explaining

You see, it's *our* snow Sir,
It's not the Tyrolean sort,
Or that found in a Swiss resort,
Or even parts of France.
It comes to us from somewhere cold
And when the year is dark and old
We like to have the chance
To have our *own* snow Sir.

We like to see it pure and fresh,
Where animal or human flesh
Have not yet ventured forth.
We thrill to hear the pundits say
"It's going to be a dreadful day,
The wind is in the north!"
And we shall have snow Sir.

I wonder if you understand
That some of us in this fair land
Are really quite at one
With Nature's way of pleasing us,
Of dropping down and freezing us;
So when our day is done—
We shall have *known* snow Sir.

Farewell

We met, my love, so long ago;
I knew you then.
Of Fate's intent we could not know;
I loved you then.
But now a fall of winter's snow
Has smothered me—
And you as well.
We lay below; you're lost to me.
Our hands may never touch again;
Apart are we.
But in the summer's gentle rain
We'll weep shall we?
No sun can ever warm to life
The joy in us;
We've suffered winter's cruel knife
Destroying us.

Maturity

When I was quite a child, I thought a tree was just a tree,
A cloud was just a floating thing, or so it seemed to me.
A meadow was a grassy place where one could gather flowers,
The sun, a warm and golden ball, that shone between the showers.

A field of waving corn was just some unseen farmer's crop,
The evening was a nuisance, for it meant that day must stop.
The sea was quite a jolly place where one could swim and play,
But sand invaded everything and rather spoilt the day.

But then I grew, as children do, and life moved on apace,
And then I found, when I turned round, a change had taken place.
No longer did I see the world as just a place to be,
My eyes had ceased from looking and at last had learned to see.

A tree no longer seems to me a tall impassive growth,
But does, for grace and dignity, exemplify them both.
Its leaves, like fingers, feel the breeze; its branches barely sway,
But bow and curtsey when the wind is ruffling up the day.

When gentle evening spreads its peace, a tree will stand compliant,
Becoming like its neighbours do, a mighty, golden giant.
It spreads its branches to the sun as if in gratitude,
How calming is this time of day, this mellow interlude.

I'd seen all this before, of course, with eyes that did not care,
The awe of winter weather with the landscape bleak and bare,
The howling wind, the slanting rain, dark streets where little stirs,
The cottages, all wet and grey, behind black conifers.

Of course, I did enjoy the snow—young people always do—
But did I see the beauty of the more extended view?
Or see the far horizon disappear in clouds of snow?
Or watch the grey flakes in the sky turn white as they fell low?

Or feel the power of the sea, when storms are in the air?
Or gaze on rippling cornfields when a gentle breeze is there?
Or see the moon with gentle light spread silver far and wide
To sparkle on the frosty ground, whilst we keep warm inside?

There is so much to wonder at, in this our island land.
One wishes youth, with lives ahead, could learn to understand.
Perhaps it needs maturity and that cannot be taught,
It seems appreciation comes when life is growing short.

Mourning

Close your eyes if the sunshine seems mockingly bright,
Close your ears to familiar sounds of the night.
Close your mind if your thoughts seem distorted with pain,
Close your heart when you know you won't see him again.

Try to smile when a bird sings a glorious song,
Understand when your days seem eternally long.
But remember the world has appointments to keep,
That it cannot stand still while we struggle and weep.

Keep your mind on the present and not on the past,
See the sun in the sky where it was overcast.
Let your sorrowing ease as you try to move on,
You will always remember the one who has gone.

Catch the world up again and return to your place,
Know your loved one is near though you can't see his face,
Be prepared for the happiness life has for you
And accept it with vigour as he wants you to.

Oxford

I went to Oxford yesterday,
A chance to visit came my way.
I saw again those ancient stones
That live forever in my bones.

I heard the bells of Magdalen
And distant others joining in;
And I heard Tom, deep, strong and proud,
Boom out above the viewing crowd.

And I saw Carfax meeting place,
Where well-known streets come face to face.
A tower, steeped in age, stands there
And people come from everywhere.

I saw the clock above the Plain;
I saw the river banks again
With overhanging willow trees
Which bring punt users to their knees.

The Cherwell still flows slowly on
As in the days for me long gone,
When youthful friends spent sunny days
Exploring Oxford's waterways.

And still they do and evermore,
To silent punt pole, splashing oar;
Where stately swans glide very near
And coot and moorhen show no fear.

A grandson caused my visit there—
A cricketer of talent rare.
I sat on Oxford's perfect green,
I heard the bells, I saw the scene.

The game, of course, came to an end,
I travelled homeward with my friend.
I went to Oxford yesterday,
But oh, alas, I could not stay.

More Utter Rubbish: Snippets from a Dance Floor

What was that flew past the door then?
Was it somebody from France?
Thought it might have been a moorhen;
Shall we dance?

Can't imagine what they're cooking,
Smells like something from the sea.
Do you think a snail's good looking?
Possibly.

Takes a while to learn a language,
Not unless your hair is pink.
Think I'll go and eat a sandwich
In the sink.

I adore to polish rabbits,
If I ever get the chance.
Don't blue cups have funny habits?
Yes, let's dance.

From a Funny Friend

"Forgive me if I trouble you,
My name begins with 'W'.
The alphabet is not my friend,
I'd rather be the other end.
Why can't I be an 'A' or 'B'?
'Twould mean an awful lot to me.
There's only 'X' and 'Y' and 'Z',
I think I'm going back to bed!"

Echoes

Why do some evenings make us sad?
Is it because of all we had?
When we were young and days were long,
And bedtime brought the blackbird's song?

We danced with laughter in our feet,
The breeze was warm, the air was sweet.
And in our lives so little rain,
And soon the sun was there again.

We built our snowmen, picked our flowers,
The waving meadows all were ours.
In hide-and-seek we hid and found
And played our hopscotch on the ground.

We spun our tops and rolled our hoops,
And there were games we played in groups.
We gave no thought to later life,
We felt no stress, we knew no strife.

And when the evening sun spread wide,
No one was sad and no one cried.
We knew the night was on its way,
Tomorrow was another day.

But now we're old, and now we cry
Deep down inside where mem'ries lie.
For now the golden evening sun
Tells us our days are nearly done.

The Little Road

That little road that leaves the main and wanders out of sight,
No signpost tells you where it goes, if it turns left or right.
The countryside it travels through is thickly green and high;
I've often wondered where it goes as I have driven by.

Sometimes I think that it could be a little private road
That leads one over cattle grids to some superb abode,
Which brings the area to life with garden teas and fêtes,
And always stands so fine and proud behind tall crested gates.

Broad steps climb upwards to the door where pillars stand each side,
With balconies and terraces and flowerbeds deep and wide.
I also see a sweeping drive and lawns that spread afar,
Where ancient oaks and cedars thrive away from bus and car.

At times a village comes to mind, unnoticed from above,
Where people live, grow old and die, and young ones fall in love.
It is a close community with church and pub and shop,
Where strangers, having lost their way, drive in but seldom stop.

They may of course look round the church or view the shop's display;
Then having purchased all they need they quickly drive away.
They then forget the village that they never meant to see
'Til faulty navigation left them drifting aimlessly.

But then another day I see a low and sprawling school,
With areas to play in and a blue and sparkling pool;
With tennis courts, a hockey pitch and netball over there;
So well arranged and organised for pupils in its care.

And then I see expensive cars move slowly up the drive;
It is a school occasion and the place has come alive.
Long strings of bunting tell the tale that this is Founders Day,
With many things prepared until the parents drive away.

But when I've finished travelling with nothing much to do,
I think about my little road and all I've put it through!
Of course, I know my hopes for it are probably in vain,
Most likely it just saunters on and joins another main.

Then the Rain Stopped

A shabby street behind the town,
With empty yards and backs of shops;
Old red-brick walls, some falling down,
And battered bins with battered tops.

A soaking day with smoke-grey sky,
The broken paving held the rain;
The gutter water trickled by
Until, somewhere, it reached a drain.

No walkers ever walked that way;
No bus stops there to travel to;
No lamps to light the end of day,
One saw no traffic passing through.

This lonely, bleak, unlovely place,
Forgotten by the local town,
Owed little to the human race,
That all could see had let it down.

Yet in this dereliction stood
A dwelling from a former time;
Dark brick and slate —no modern wood—
High windows, both opaque with grime.

It stood, a lonely sentinel,
No longer proud but wet and sad.
Perhaps a storehouse, who could tell?
Long gone the love that once it had.

But as I turned to wander on,
I noticed sunshine warming me,
And suddenly the rain had gone,
No grey clouds threatened stormily.

And now the gloomy street was bright,
I never had expected this.
The soaking pavements gleamed with light—
A total metamorphosis.

And as I stood, one more surprise:
The gate beside the old house swung.
A man and wife with happy eyes
Looked up to where the clouds had hung.

Then hand in hand and warmly gloved
They walked away with steady gait.
And now I knew the house was loved,
I thought to go—I would not wait.

I felt intrusive standing there,
I had no part in this scene's life.
Now I must leave the house in care
By one old man and his dear wife.

The Splodge

We once had a splodge as a guest
Who seemed absolutely obsessed
With eating the carpets, devouring his bed,
Until on his twenty-first morning he said
"I'm sorry, I really do feel
I must have a sizeable meal;
I've eaten the curtains, the chairs and the mats;
I've eaten five pigeons, three dogs and four cats.
And now there is nothing to try,
I must, with regret, say goodbye.

Twilight

I felt no fear when darkness fell,
When as a child I lay in bed;
But I remember very well
The twilight made me hide my head.

But why remained a mystery
Until I reached my autumn years,
When ageing eyes revealed to me
The reasons for my childhood fears.

My bedroom window showed tall trees;
An orchard of the unpruned kind.
Old friends, well known to me were these,
Where chickens strutted unconfined.

Their owner came each day with feed,
A kind old man in smock and yoke;
Two buckets hung both full of seed—
The custom then with country folk.

A road ran by, but cars were few;
Ideal for hopscotch, whipping tops,
And all the things that children do
'Til bedtime comes and playtime stops.

But I grew up and left that place
And all my childhood fears behind.
Then one day I came face to face
With what had so disturbed my mind.

I passed some trees one eventide
And glanced to where they met the sky.
A sudden stab of fear inside
Transported me to times gone by.

I was that child again in bed;
Outside my window tall trees grew.
I lay there covering my head
For reasons that at last I knew.

But one thing I may never know;
How fearsome did those trees appear
To frighten me so long ago
When twilight came and night drew near.

Were branches then ferocious claws
That grabbed the sky and threatened me?
Would I be torn by bloody jaws
And then devoured voraciously?

I do not think I want to know
Unless some nightmare forces me.
But twilight trees will ever show
Just what provoked my fantasy.

Two Muddled Old Men

"That ball in? No it's not."
"What a shame, smashing shot."
"But the goalie was there—
Seemed to fly through the air."
"Someone's down on the ground,
Lots of chaps standing round,
Maiden over maybe?"
"I don't know, I can't see."
"Both the umpires have come,
Must say, one's looking glum!"
"Now the stretcher's come on;
Oh! The player has gone—
Down to square leg I think,
Someone's passed him a drink."
"Now he's going to bowl;
Time the ball got to roll!"
"Oh! He *is* good at that—
That tall chap with the hat.
Hit it right in the net,
One he'll never forget."
"What was that someone cried?
Was he really offside?"
"They called 'over' old chum
And we've only just come!"
"It's not over at all,
Someone's just kicked the ball."
"Oh I don't understand.
Why's the ball in his hand?"
"Oh that goalie's a menace!
Let's go and watch tennis."

Water Please

Oh water-can, do please help me,
My soil's as dry as it can be.
Quite dead I look, and come the day
They'll throw my pot and me away.

And I have leaves as yet unfurled,
I want to show them to the world.
They're pretty leaves and dainty too;
Oh dear! I don't know what to do.

Oh thank you, now I'm feeling well,
You've poured on water I can tell.
It's running down among my roots,
Refreshing all my dying shoots.

Oh lovely! Now here comes the dawn,
And I, at last, am not forlorn;
Some sun on me will help no end,
Dear water-can you are my friend.

Tongue in Cheek

With trees in my garden and woods all around,
The wind in these trees makes a wonderful sound.
I live in a dwelling of which I'm so fond,
But better than these, there's a frog in my pond.

The views from my windows make everyone smile;
They stretch over countryside mile after mile.
I live here in comfort with my little dog,
My life is complete now my pond has a frog.

Maybe I'm foolish to feel such delight;
My garden is just the most terrible sight,
With weeds in profusion and brambles beyond,
I really don't mind—there's a frog in my pond.

A Conversation with an Old Lady

Now here I can no longer stay,
The time has come to move away.
"A home" I heard the lady say,
When she was here the other day.

She also said "She'll have to share,
There are no single rooms to spare;
But I am sure she'll settle there
With all the other folk in care."

She sat and chattered on her 'phone,
I didn't like her bossy tone;
"She really must not live alone,
She cannot cope here on her own."

Can't cope indeed! What does she mean?
She doesn't know, she hasn't seen;
My mind may not be quite so keen,
But I am old, not seventeen.

I shall not see my roses bloom,
Nor smell their heady, sweet perfume,
For I must go and share a room,
A thought that fills my head with gloom.

I'll never see my home again,
I don't need telling, that's quite plain;
If only they could share my pain,
They'd change their minds – let me remain.

And now the plans have all been laid,
Can no one see that I'm afraid?
To leave this cherished home I've made,
That I shall love 'til memories fade.

Evening

So many years of memories live in an evening sky,
When daytime's battles with the world have slid behind the trees;
A moment then of loneliness when no one passes by,
And that is when you shed the tear that no one ever sees.

Forty ✒

Shepherd your shadows and take them to market;
Sell them to summer who knows what to do.
Retrace your steps on a soft mossy carpet;
Do not let old mem'ries make shadows for you.

Lightning Source UK Ltd.
Milton Keynes UK
UKOW051225070412

190291UK00001B/36/P